the memory of water

the memory of water

poems

Brendan McBreen

MoonPath Press

Copyright © 2022 Brendan McBreen
All rights reserved.

No part of this publication may be reproduced, distributed, or transmitted in any form or by any means whatsoever without written permission from the publisher, except in the case of brief excerpts for critical reviews and articles. All inquiries should be addressed to MoonPath Press.

Poetry
ISBN 978-1-936657-70-4

Front Cover photo: Swimming Skyward by James Rodgers

Author photo by Brendan McBreen

Book design by Tonya Namura, using
Colaborate-Thin (display) and Minion Pro (text).

MoonPath Press, an imprint of Concrete Wolf Poetry Series,
is dedicated to publishing the finest poets
living in the U.S. Pacific Northwest.

MoonPath Press
PO Box 445
Tillamook, OR 97141

MoonPathPress@gmail.com

http://MoonPathPress.com

acknowledgments

The author gratefully acknowledges and thanks the following publications where some of the poems in this collection previously appeared.

Auburn Examiner: "A bird in the hand"

The Bosch and Bruegel Poetry Ekphrastic Anthology: "What the wind foretells is not always truth"

Chrome Baby: "It's been three weeks," "Sandy"

Discretionary Love: "Shape"

Espial: "50% off"

Exterminating Angel: "Once"

Haiku Universe: "the bend"

Mad Swirl: "Sometimes the squirrels," "Things to do while waiting for the apocalypse"

Soul Lit: "There is a particular kind of brilliance"

Star*line: "Ten dinosaurs"

gratitude

Gratitude and love to my dad, the Poet Laureate of Pacific WA, Gerald A. McBreen (2/7/1936 - 5/17/2022) who insisted the TV be turned off twice a week so he could read to myself and my brother. He gave me Frankenstein, King Kong and Ray Bradbury and I am eternally grateful.

Special thanks to Lana, Kitt, Deb, Sherry, and John from our Friday writing group. You are all such inspirations and wonderful writers! Many of the poems in this collection owe their existence to you.

Appreciation to Striped Water Poets and Northwest Renaissance: Poets, Performers & Publishers. And thanks to everyone who reads, listens to, and writes poetry.

Contents

i. our natural lives
communion	5
anachronism of starlight	6
feather of a broken oracle	8
sometimes squirrels	10
living our natural lives	11
emerald moss	12
the smiling particle	14
yard work	15
there is a particular kind of brilliance	18
moonless night	19
a rose	20
the bend	22

ii. we will not go gently
ten dinosaurs	25
birds will flock	26
who will you be when you are no longer you?	27
how desperately I wanted to be found out	29
now	30
we were not here first, we will not be here last	31
if we saw them, we'd think they were robots	32
we will not go gently	34
once	36
the old folks talk of sky	38
it's been three weeks	39

iii. nine times
purple dead nettle	43
what the wind foretells is not always truth	45
children are burning	47
worth more than gold	48
chicken soup	50
politics	52
dragonfly	55

trouble went walking	57
Jesus is	58
Product Safety Information	59
nine times	60
mass shootings	62
dead girl	64
marching on	66
I want to be anyone except me today	67
he refuses all fear	69
gathering dust	71
the decision	72

iv. nonexistent time

interview with some guy who doesn't know what pigs are	77
the cows of tomorrow	78
all the kids knew	80
fear	81
it was a long dull flight	83
tweeting tern	84
my stop?	85
the leaves are looking at me	86
should've got a dog	87
what would you say	89
loss swirls in blue syncopation	90
as a child	91
blind oracles peruse my dreams	92
that night	93
nonexistent time	95
rejection	97
as an editor	98
have you ever noticed	99
the naturopath	100
50% off	101
when your laundry by the door	102
throwing myself away	103
long ago	104

room 12	105
a mask for every occasion	107
Sandy	108
in love with love	109
Howard's favorite rock	110
it was in the back seat	112
Chill	113
loud music filled the room	114
shapes	115
I remember a gap	116

v. what is what seems

some things I love	121
forget-me-not	122
behind the door was	123
trucks and truck parts	124
cages we choose	125
a recipe	126
the angry onion	127
kittens	128
a bird in the hand	129
as a poet	131
what is what seems	133
light unknown	135
Wonderful World	137
shadow and light	139
does the memory of water	140
things to do while waiting for the apocalypse	141
things I have forgotten	142
dandelions	143
tonight	144
all through this night	145
Today's Sermon	146
I don't have any answers	148
about the author	151

the memory of water

i. our natural lives

communion

floating

in starlight

otters
hold hands

so not to drift
apart

while dreaming
of shells

and all
that might be found

deeper

anachronism of starlight

falls
fades
in dawn

two deer

watch

whatever there is
to see
hear
feel

they are
landscape
in this
primal painting

pigment
in fury
of brushes
being
belonging

between
star birth
and the
glint
in the eyes
of two deer

some say
falling
is just finding
the self
of ground

feather of a broken oracle
after Denise Levertov

the blowing
of air alone
is not wind

movement
of molecules
is heat

shape is life

time
doesn't exist

Ma'at
measures
the immeasurable
one feather
at a time

hearts
of stone
hearts of light
ring clear
from scales

one feather
no matter
how heavy
is not a wing

flight
is how birds
express their love
to the wind

sometimes squirrels

teleport entire vending machines

into holes in willows

all the while
acting innocent

no one wants to confront them

who knows
where
you'd end up

living our natural lives

on this salty wet rock
spinning lonely
amid dust
and whatever
isn't quite void enough
to non-exist

natural lives
but who wants that?

access to indoor plumbing
elastic
cars and explosions on TV
we want
plastic vaccines
plastic canned food
plastic
in our new joints
natural
is natural
as rot
we want
to shine
burn out
young
beautiful
enigmatic
to alien
archaeologists
who only know
us
by our plastic
mannequins

emerald moss

stains
my foggy memory

I thought it was
a green
earth-bound
cloud
soft
spongy
bitter cotton candy
catching rain drops
like stars
or frozen fireworks

the more I looked
the more I found
this luscious life
a world of its own
complete with orange dragons
crawling within

mesmerized
the idea didn't flee my mind
a whole week
of school
and family

later
Saturday
in a sun beam
I was still drawing
the micro world I'd seen
or imagined
savory foliage

hiding everything
from dinosaurs
to robots
to goldfish
and white crowned sparrows
each layer
deeper into the amazing
but the more I drew
the more mundane
it became
albeit
still surreal
recognizable buildings
mixed with giant moss
orange reptiles
old tires
on and on
layer after layer
until
I recognized even more
a circle
mostly blue
coastline
a house
a window
and me
drawing
all reality
whole universes
in my sketchbook

the smiling particle

leaps from
place to place
unheeding any consequences

now in a pomegranate
now with some smog

it tesseracts
in simultaneous
moments
here there
then tomorrow

all the while smiling

believing
physicists
will never catch it

yard work

wind
dances
tall grass

dandelions
open yellow eyes
to the sun

now overcast
ladybugs
explore
every leaf
every blade
serrated edge
and flower

ivy hides
wonders
beneath
the thirsty
stary veins
of its leaves

purple dead nettle
clover
buttercups
forget-me-nots
bluebells
mint
and others
I have
no names for
embrace
the earth

which would
otherwise
be barren

it may
be fallow
overgrown
gone wild
but the sparrows
the robins
and blue-jays
have no complaints

ladybugs
and bees
signal
their spotted
and striped
Thank Yous
and yes
I am also
lazy

I prefer
watching
leaves wave
exploring
for hidden lives
dancing within
to plowing
it all down

I prefer
life
growing

the only weed
a rusty
lawnmower
tangled
with vine

there is a particular kind of brilliance

involved
in being a hummingbird
starving for sugar-water
glistening
with impossible to track
wingbeats
sparkly feathers
your only job
to delight
the eye
of any passer-by
it is enough
to hover
in a world too slow
to catch you
to drink
from the finest
most flamboyant
of natural cups
to live among flowers
and jewels of dew
there is a particular
kind of brilliance
just watching a hummingbird
as if being
in the present moment
and observing beauty
were your only job

moonless night

echoes off walls
without pictures

a rose

falls away
petal
by petal
until the grass
below
is a celebration
of pink confetti

oblivious to time's
onward cycling
robins hunt for worms
while clouds popcorn the sky
and monarchs brighten by

soon new greens
will fade darker
red robins
will be replaced
by red leaves
the sky with gray
and the rose
will keep only its thorns

next Spring
is but a dream
an imagined possibility
that may
or may not exist

but right now
the petals which remain
the pleasant heat
cool breeze
and moist earth

are all that matters
all that is
all a rose knows

the bend

in the buttercup's stem
and then
the bumblebee
moves on

ii. we will not go gently

ten dinosaurs

were found fully intact
in the gas tank
of a Chevrolet
in Cleveland
Tuesday

oil executives
lamented the situation
saying they should
have charged extra

birds will flock

with whomever
they damn well please

gay penguins adopting an egg

black and gold hawks
different species
different genus entirely
making adorable hybrids

nature doesn't conform
to human bigotry

who will you be when you are no longer you?

overexposed
seagulls
in Hitchcockian swarm
how mono-maniacs
polarize
every and any thing
no matter how neutral
or irrelevant
twisted
into cannon fodder
for their singular cause

maybe Hitchcock was right
the birds are better off without us
this polarization
of even light itself
making simple reality
a lie

as if reality
was simple
or indeed
the only truth

but seagulls
caught static
in neutrally buoyant
wind
did not ask
to be polarized
nor do they care

humans will take
care of themselves

without
any avian
intervention

so the birds
the birds
birds birds birds birds
birds
the cawing and clawing
of the birds
goes on
regardless
of which polarity
people want to imprint
upon this particular pic

how desperately I wanted to be found out

the seed of a weed
under all that dirt
I wanted sunlight
to be touched
by rain
understood

I struggled
up through the minutiae
of time and rust
sprouted one leaf
to the overcast
and too swiftly learned
how constricting
a pot can be

how some people
always need something
to prune

now

even on mars
plastic

we were not here first, we will not be here last
after Jeannine Hall Gailey

waves
become fire
in the Fukushima Sea
while
unnamed
life
sinks
to the deep
burning ooze
of
radioactive dreams

if we saw them, we'd think they were robots

when the deepest microbes
finally emerge
to find
even the death of decay
choked away
by micro-plastics

they will evolve
adapt
to the new paradigm
as life does

organic polymers
will raise forests
of living plastic tendrils

slowly
they will diversify
spread
throughout the planet
incorporate new minerals
new chemical processes

one day
a consciousness
much like ours will emerge

but humans
will be long extinct
long forgotten

and these new beings
will speculate
endlessly

but never truly know
where the plastics
of their origin
came from

we will not go gently

into that
good night
we will
kick and
scream
hydrogen sutras
to the end of ends
remake
a glowing microbial genome
complete
with peons to plastic
petrochemical Paradise
an Eden
for survivors
to adapt
mutate
and grow
into unimagined
morphologies
of ecology
too toxic
for human meat

but life

evolution

will persist

and one day
our wandering spirits
may find new

corpus antenna
capable of receiving
our ethereal selves

will we
destroy it all
yet again?

once

people would gather food
and store it in little towers
these little towers dotted the landscape
and all was plentiful

after a time
some of these towers
were combined
into one big tower
and it kept gobbling up the other towers
until it was the only one left

no one had enough to eat
no new clothes
houses crumbled
but soon enough
the big tower fell
and everyone had enough again
and went back to making many little towers

however
in time
the little towers were merged again
and people suffered

then
as before
this tower fell
and people prospered

then later
the little towers
were once more
merged into a single tower

this time
reaching higher
than anyone had seen before
again
people were without
they cried and wailed
but the tower
would not fall

soon
the people were
so hungry
they all turned to salt
and the land
turned to salt

and there was no one left
except
one angry little boy
on top of the crumbling tower
one mean little boy
throwing rocks
at birds

the old folks talk of sky

or some other ancient mythology

like when people actually owned things

how crazy is that!

people owning things

even if that was
the way it was back then

how chaotic it must have been

so much better
being a commodity

so much simpler
renting clothes
having them upgraded
and customized
within your earnings potential

no one needs to stand out
be uncomfortable

those old folks
must have had it tough

with no one
to tell them
how to live

it's been three weeks

since the portal to Hell
opened up
in our back yard

we've gotten used to it

even Grandma

she met a fiery arch-demon
she trades recipes with

we have to make substitutions though

like instead of the souls of un-baptized children

we use kale

iii. nine times

purple dead nettle

blood purple leaves
of a weed looks like a pagoda
with pink flowers
on the roof

I remember weeds
fascinating
how they would strive
upward
sometimes branching about
with little white bundles
of flowers at the top

I always thought
it would be neat
if the weeds
were as tall as trees

but they would always get
ripped out
and replaced
with homogenous length swathes of grass

and I would be scolded
for making riverbanks
with the expensive hose water

as I grew up
I learned
people can be weeds too

some too dark to fit in
others too colorful

I figured out quickly
standing out
was dangerous

what the wind foretells is not always truth
*after The Garden of Earthly Delights,
Hieronymus Bosch*

to see
with the skin
of your skin

uncovered
we are all made of light

burning
without burning

our animal selves
build temples
lurid among stamen

dancing
to an inverted aria
disjointed waltz

a song
on the threshold
of something more
than madness
ecstasy

grandeur
among falling time

degraded passion
imprisoned symphony
sympathy
which does not rise
beyond

the limp numbness
of it all

is this where we find
our fate?

these ruins
blossoming
with the impurest
of intentions

or are we
some other animal

unnamed

unintended

just
passing through

children are burning

in cages
viral
and hidden

their mouths
too full
of non-English words

there are
butterflies
even in Hell

worth more than gold

Business Insider says:

cocaine
heroin
platinum
rhodium
diamonds
LSD
hafnium and tantalum isomers
(cooling rods for nuclear reactors)
and
antimatter

I'd say:

happiness
contentment
love
humor
connections
a healthy environment
a healthy ecosystem
peace of mind
joy in artistic expression
being wholly and unconditionally
    accepted for who one is
being awestruck
    by the marvels of nature
    the ingenuity of science
    the near perfection
    of a piece of art
    the ideal song to fit the moment

having enough to eat
not having to fear one's neighbors
not living in the shadow of violence
kittens
laughing with friends
moonlight
being safe and warm
watching a storm at sea

chicken soup

isn't good
for the chicken

the sun shines
burns near forever
boiling
at a million plus degrees

shall we talk
about
the lucky
rabbit foot

or the rainbow
light
being shattered
by a drop
of water

every silver lining
has
its dark clouds

modern medicine
technology
micro-plastics
industrial waste

you want
a house in the woods
you have
to cut down the trees

beautiful
wildlife
hungry
full of parasites

maybe they are right
when they say
ignorance
is bliss

if you ignore
the chicken's fate
the soup
is pretty good

politics

Hungry Ghosts
choking
on cell phones
oblivious
to where
they are driving

angel wings
of smog
beckon
our lungs
to join
dying trees
rotting
and glowing
in wormy syncopation
with Lunar indifference

tides surround me
wash away
my compassion
rust my gratitude
and I don't accept Hate
I don't accept indifference

drivers
like ants
scurrying
through their scurry lives

yes
we all have to live

except Ukrainians
except Black people
Pagans
Trans women and men
Gay people
Women
under Taliban control
not even allowed to scurry

the rats
have eaten the heads
off all our chocolate bunnies
and buried our leaders
in their excrement

drivers swerve
to miss them
swirling around
a labyrinth
leading
to un-enlightenment
and more scurrying
shitting microplastics
into the ocean
swallowing every shiny con
forced into their lines of sight

all the while
sewage levels
rise
air disappears

while mass murderers
and mass producers
ignore it all
on personal floatation devices

sipping designer urine
(sixty thousand dollars per bottle)
discussing ways
to increase
people's debt
and whether it is possible
to tax the dead

dragonfly

cherry trees
open their eyes
pink
        pearl
                white
snow
wind petals
in drying Spring
pollinated air

you talk
of peace
relatives
fluffy clouds
and gates

ask me
what do I think happens
when we die

watching
each cherry petal
exist
in its own moment

I think
a thousand years
from now
the nuclear holy war
between
those who believe
the Great God Oprah
is a middle aged white man
like themselves

and those
who believe in history
will finally
be the end
of humanity

sometime after that
I'll be reincarnated
as a dragonfly

trouble went walking

found clover
and talked
about luck
and the gunshot wounds
everyone seems to be getting these days
more popular than body piercings
but no one
wants to shoot trouble
and clover
has enough problems
with lawn mowers

Jesus is

Jesus is Black

Jesus is Middle Eastern

Jesus is fiction

Jesus is pissed off
        by what evil people
        do in His name

Product Safety Information

firearms

This product can be lethal if used incorrectly.
This product can be lethal if used correctly.

This product is not appropriate for people
frightened of other races or gender expressions.

Keep out of reach of
childish people
who blame their problems on scapegoats.

Product not intended
for those with the emotional maturity
of a two-year-old.

Do not use this product
if you are ending a relationship
or planning on ending one soon.

Use of this product in conjunction with
drugs and alcohol
or general stupidity is not recommended.

nine times

music was playing
by itself
when
nine times
day ended
too soon
nine times
he will kick our sandcastle down
until we agree
he is better
we are inferior

nine times
we smile
rebuild
disagree

nine times
gunshots
ring out
blood stops flowing
light disappears
nine times
strange fruit
sway
a crow calls

nine times
a uniform
makes someone right

nine times
we are told
it's not about race

an old ship enters harbor
the familiar stench
of dread and decay

nine times
we say never again
not today

nine times
nine more funerals

but the doors
are still open
the music
is still playing
and nine more times
the dead
forgive
the living

mass shootings

when I was in grade school
no one ever told me
someone
might show up one day
and shoot us all

somehow
I missed that lesson

what happened
between back then
and now?
what pollutant
in our ecosystem
causes such toxic insanity?

or is this nothing new?

did the same people
shooting up schools today
lynch black people in the 50s?
are they the same ones
who fired up the furnaces
in 1940s Germany?
are they Indian hunters?
Slavers?
are they the same ones
promoting new religion
by killing followers of the old?
the heirs of the Roman legions?
Sparta?
Cain?

has there ever
been a time
when people
didn't murder each other?

dead girl

the dead girl
watches the world
with hollow eyes

it is the birth of winter
the overcast
dark and full

this dead girl died
because her family found out
she loved the wrong person

another
in Buenos Aires
simply because the men
were done with her

in Juarez three generations
gone at once

across the U.S.
disappeared Indian girls
wonder if they are dead yet

in my own town
formerly called Slaughter
one resident left a trail
along the Green River
a connect-the-dots of dead girls
a scavenger hunt for crows

the call and response of thunder
shakes the air
and rain

finally lets go
of the sky

sometimes
I wonder
how the world would look
how now would be different
if all those women
were still alive

marching on

thinking about
the distortions
and manipulations
of tyrants
and want-to-be tyrants
I was watching sparrows
forage for their lunch
in my back yard
and realized
even this
could be twisted
into something political

the invasion of Ukraine
is only happening on a screen for me
I can't relate
to having my home blown up
my city leveled
people I know
being murdered
and then some tyrant blaming me
for his choices
I don't know what being invaded is like

but
I do have ants in my kitchen
they keep coming back again and again
have no respect
for my life
or property
taking what doesn't belong to them
do the ants justify their behavior
by claiming they are just following the whims
of the one in charge?

I want to be anyone except me today

to not be alone
to not
worry
someone will kill me
just for being me
I am always afraid
someone will see through
my disguise
watching carefully
counting the people
as they go in
and out
of the restroom
if I am quick
I can get in and out
while it's empty
just in case
someone notices
my lacy undies
and decides to shoot me

pretend
to be a man
practice
walking like a guy
sitting like a guy
hating myself
for knowing
just what to say
in guy-talk
to blend in
disappear
to be one of them
longing for her figure

for the comport
of how they interact with each other
but agreeing
every time
yeah, she's a hottie
no not a 10
but still

sometimes I wonder what
it would be like
to face my fear
to have someone
pull a gun on me
it might be a relief
finally
a way out

he refuses all fear

proud of his courage
he continues
the tirade
he tells them
in no uncertain terms
what he thinks of them

and then
unsure what to do next
works up to yelling
absolutely sure
he'll win the argument

so focused
on winning
on stating his point
he doesn't know how or where to stop

so he escalates

oblivious
to his audience
except that they are there

he jabs his finger
shakes his fist
and caresses his open carry side arm

but again
now what to do?

oops!
someone is trying to say something
he can't let that happen
he has to win

time to scream louder
push and shove a little
escalate

he caresses his gun
with no idea
where it is all leading

gathering dust

I'd like to destroy
every gun manufacturer
in the world

I'd like to destroy them
financially

and then
provide
all the public services
any homeless person
could need or want

I'd like guns
to be an anachronism

found only in museums

a strange and bizarre relic
from a time
no one wants to return to

the decision

it was a deer
one said

it was an antelope
said the other

ants can't elope

I said antelope not cantaloupe

no it was a deer

the argument went on like this
for four days

finally it was decided
(by whom no one cares to admit)
that neither position
could be correct
unless the other was wrong
and to figure
which argument was correct
the arguers should both
try to kill each other
with chop-sticks
the one left alive
would of course be correct

it was the only civilized solution

off in the distance
just past the tree line
a deer and an antelope watch

thanking their various gods
that they
are not civilized

iv. nonexistent time

interview with some guy who doesn't know what pigs are

I forget what I even asked

but he responded sarcastically
yeah right, when pigs walk!

this got my attention

you mean *when pigs fly*, I suggested

huh, he said, *no birds fly, pigs just float around in mud*

um, you do know what pigs are don't you?

of course I do!
pigs are a kind of microscopic organism which farmers bred really big
in order to collect the hazardous feces and threaten the local drinking water
and thereby collect extortion money from the government

this was not the answer I expected

when I composed myself
I asked, *in that case where does bacon come from?*

sweat shop labor
yep, they use turkeys to manufacture it
there is a warning right on the package
it says turkey bacon
you should never buy that kind
most of those turkeys are treated horribly
you know they're just praying for Thanksgiving

the cows of tomorrow

nobody really knows just when
the cows will come home
tomorrow maybe
or next Tuesday

somehow
the moon looks different
with forty-seven million people living on it
these people dream
distant memories
of being tethered
by denser gravity
green memories
sacred water
forest cathedrals
before mine waste
war and pollution
recast the atmosphere
into brown-orange sludge

cows and people
the only animals able to survive
in moon domes and tunnels
now that the Earth
is a perpetual fireworks display
of rusted ordinance
and greenhouse gas

but the moon is livable enough
and the grassy moss lichen
the cows love so much

grows everywhere
in the deeper tunnels
the cows will turn up eventually
after all
there is nowhere else to go

all the kids knew

there was a giant python
living under the slide
no one minded
it only ate once every six months
and it was easy enough to avoid

on the swings
it would move its head parallel to your back-and-forth rhythm
like it was hypnotized or something
all you had to do was swing for a bit
then jump off and run away

the merry-go-round was easy too
you just need to get it spinning fast
then jump on and stay in the middle
when the snake sticks its head in
it gets whacked over and over by the hand rails
and slithers away discouraged

the kids on the teeter-totters though
well
they're doomed

fear

God's boss is a red car
or a slug drowned in booze

I want fear to understand
I am not intimidated
fear doesn't scare me as much anymore

the melancholy fly
buzzing my ear
understands
for different reasons

fear
has a face like hashbrowns
or the moon
a face
the fly rushes to meet
and retreats in numbness and grief

I do fear grief
I'd travel to the rain
to avoid remorse

once in a book
the fly found love
I found my journal
and a tiger
strolling and carousing
the rocky neighborhood

the thing about fear is
its only as big
or as small
as imagination

like God
the grease-monkey under the hood
of the cherry Corolla
or a drunk slug
afraid
of nothing

it was a long dull flight

and it wasn't over
I glanced across the isle
at the little girl sitting there
she was absorbed in some type of game
she held an over-sized remote control device
and I started to notice
every time she moved it left
the plane banked left
when she shook it
turbulence
in shock I realized
through some kind of technological fluke
this seven or eight year old
was actually flying the plane
then I noticed
the girl was looking back at me
I put my seat belt on
and tightened it
then asked
can you do a barrel roll?

tweeting tern

turns in the air
closing closer to her wake
racing the sunset
higher and higher
saying goodbye
to the ocean
hi to the sky
the scent of flower fades
as this wonder ascends
beyond the view
from the unpolished window
hey! someone shouts
the light is green
and there are packages to ship
people to meet
and loose change
in love
rattling across the floor

my stop?

What are you waiting for! she said
not a question an accusation
I'm not sure if this is my stop or not I said
look just get off the bus or stay on,
I have a schedule to keep
Okay I said

I stepped off
into the cold rain
conscious of how close the bus was
as it growled away from me
this place
was unfamiliar
the shopping center
with oddly named stores
the models of cars
even the people and their clothes
where am I? I muttered

Mars!
a grizzled gray bearded hermit
in mismatched stained clothes said
You're on Mars
and this is MY stop!
he yelled
before turning to rummage through
an overfilled shopping cart

I moved on quickly
I knew the streets
the layout
but I was more sure than ever
this place
was no longer home

the leaves are looking at me

is it any wonder
I've fallen apart
become disassembled
mulch
for the forest around me
all my pencils
broken
no sharpeners
only crisp brown
regret
piling in upon me

a place
for bees
to keep warm
before snow comes
erasing
even my self-pity
under a ridged hug

will flowers
eventually bloom from me
or at least mushrooms
will anything
left of me
be recognizable
in the bewildering Spring?

should've got a dog

Pineapple Butt

she always calls me that
when she's worried about me

so I took the noose off
and said
it's okay, I'm just practicing

practicing for what? she asked
arching that one eyebrow

I've always wanted to be in a shrimp cocktail
I said

okay… she said
but anyway
come over here and lie down
my arm is getting tired

sure I said *is that a guillotine?*

just then she let go of the rope
severing my two longest hairs

darn it! she said
I told you my arm was tired

I'm sorry I said

maybe we could play Russian Roulette
she said

we only have two bullets
I said
what about the dog

silly! she said *we don't have a dog!*

anyway
we both missed
and decided to see other people

what would you say

*if I told you
you are a terrible
plumber?*
she said

I sloshed out
from beneath
the sink
amid a whiff
of mildew
and wet denim
looked at her
square in her
green eyes
and

the pipe burst

drenching us both
she held
her hands
to the spray
with a pronounced
eek!

the water was cool
and refreshing
on such a humid day

I gave up
and said
I'd probably agree with you

loss swirls in blue syncopation

the snow is gone
the light is golden
but ice remains
and wind
swirling in *Starry Night* rhythms

crescendos of bi-lingual howling
reverberate across the globe
echoes and images of a despot
and his army invading Ukraine
blood
bombs
rubble
refugees

at home the gold is gone
out my window
the wind is furious
and icy rain drums my roof
with a frantic rhythmless fugu
I am hungry
so I microwave a burrito

as a child

you thought the racoon
at your window
the devil

and gave her
your soul

she nurtured it
as one of her own cubs
taught it to survive
and steal
be curious and bold
even if the world hates you

you never thanked her
never called her mother

never forgave
her kindness

blind oracles peruse my dreams

on wings of fire
and Autumn leaves
bloody bandaged eye sockets
smile
at my squirming

the dark
doesn't fear me
they say

burn away
glistening
white bones
explode
radioactive
visions
of despair

skeletal hands
reach up from a circular floor
and my dream shatters

amid screaming
laughter
a million butterfly wings
wilt
as they fall

was it so much to ask
to be loved?

that night

I was happy
for the first time in a while

cauliflower made me happy

strange
I hadn't eaten cauliflower
since our *Polar expedition*
as you called it

hiking in the mountains
hoping to see a zebra
even though it was the wrong continent
and a seemingly impromptu barbecue

we roasted cauliflower of all things
amid the circumlocution of crows
and other birds
vying for someone's attention

later
separated by the tempest of our lives
and your dream job
now hiring
but all the way in Portugal

and you
not forgotten
but not really paid attention to

until now

just some quick
microwave lunch

made me stop
made me smile

nonexistent time

moments
making
snowflakes
scissors so dull
the paper wins

murmuring of Beethoven
light
everywhere

back then
in trees
whirligigs
spun
spin

she was there
Hawaiian
Polynesian
olive-gold skin
blends
well
in
memory
re
-membering

amazing

I didn't quite
love her
wanted

to
be
her

coloring
inside the lines
heavier
crayon
tracing
the lines

I can't
think
of
anything
I learned
in grade school
more
than disappointment

rejection

I am sorry to say
we will not be accepting
your submission at this time
this is not a reflection of your effort
but rather an indication
of our own gross incompetence
yes
we could not tell quality writing
from crusty gum under a bus seat
we really have no idea
what is good or bad
we simply pick submissions randomly
and hope our readers are as dumb as we are
thank you for submitting to us though
it makes us feel like we are doing something right
and please send us more of your writing
it helps us get grants

as an editor

of a small press journal, she
always has issues

have you ever noticed

there is never
a neurosurgeon
around

when you want
unnecessary
brain surgery?

the naturopath

anesthesiologist
prefers bludgeoning

50% off

s
al
e
!
plus
size
clo
th
in
g
su
chs
kinn
yma
nn
e
q
u
i
n
s
.
.
.

when your laundry by the door

is shaped like a dinosaur
it's time to wash and neaten
before you end up eaten

throwing myself away

one toenail
at a time

long ago

before I saw
the sea's heartbeat
in ocean waves
conifers near
the beach
floating
like angels
passing too quickly

before I became
a face
in shadow
an hourglass
all sand gone
a millennia ago
I was a sunrise
headed to
a fortune teller

I was in need
of a dream

she told me
she could see me in a red hoodie
surrounded by praying women
a green bell-pepper
my only possession
I don't know what this meant
I had more questions
but my time was limited
and accordion music
was beginning to follow me

room 12

I guess
if I had
a clock
it would only make it worse
but I didn't
bring my phone
just my pen and paper
I feel safer
sketching my mind
than surfing the web
or playing a game
though
I like games
getting lost
in a world
of someone else's imagining
challenging puzzles
gorgeous artwork
curious music
engaging storylines

but now
is not the place for escape
the ER is a reality to face
though I try to make my own
live in the field
of my choosing
flesh is flesh
and insurance is insurance
these fields
intersect
Venn diagram

bubble universes
in Shiva's
bathwater

the beeps and buzzes
hums and slow-motion time
are now
as eternal
as the tightness
of the ekg stickers
hugging their own
patches of my skin
here I am
if I exist
in a world plastic coated
and alive

a mask for every occasion

read the sign in the window

I walked in
asked the freckled clerk
if she had a mask to wear
for signing a peace treaty
on an alien planet

she produced
a tall striped
bit of barnacle covered wood
with three eye holes

how about a mask
for biting a tiger

she pointed to the tiger biting aisle

okay I said
show me a mask
for selling masks

she took off her freckled face

I went home
with a mask
that made me look wiser

Sandy

Sandy used to love shellfish

but one night

she had a dream
a crab was talking to her
and an oyster threatened to sue

the last time we took her to a seafood restaurant
she screamed at the clams
and ran out through traffic
waving her arms
chanting Tibetan sutras

now she's living in a log cabin
somewhere deep in the woods

she's a vegetarian
and writes historical romance novels

except
her main characters
are all lobsters

in love with love

I asked you
to carry me
to the moon

you showed me
your Medusa hair

and carved a rocket
out of the rock
I had become

Howard's favorite rock

was a chunk of granite

he believed if he talked to it regularly
the rock would learn to speak

so Howard talked to his rock

at least four hours a day
telling it anything he could think of to say

eventually
Howard died

and the rock

was sold to a short couple

but they were frightened
when the rock
began to speak

at first it complained
the couple didn't talk to it enough
then it started reciting favorite stories heard from Howard

the couple didn't know what to do
so they called three exorcists

the first two ran away

the third
stayed long after dusk

when he emerged
he told the couple
he couldn't find a rock

there was only a small child
who wanted to be called Howard Junior

it was in the back seat

of the beat up
sky blue
Honda Civic

wedged
between
the seat
and the backrest

there were
melted M&Ms
down there too

I'm sorry

I didn't know

they were
your lucky pair

Chill

holding your hand
I found
I could not bear it
any longer

I had to shout
to sing
to tell the whole world
your fingers are cold

I'm sorry
you said

tears turning to snow

you let go
of my hand

now I'm colder than ever

loud music filled the room

with flowers of smoke
and light

we danced
until our bodies ached

then danced
until we could feel
our bodies
no more

when the music
finally stopped
we went outside
into chill moonlight
and danced
to the music
still echoing
in our hearts

our bodies rose
slowly from the ground

clouds obscured the moon

and in new falling snow
we danced
into the sky

shapes

come apart
everything we see
reminds us
of clouds

once
there was a tiny man
who rode dragonflies
but one day
he grew wheels
and never left the land again

I don't want us
to be like the clouds
forever
drifting
apart

never touching
all the sky
between us

I remember a gap

between
a grassy field ringed by distant trees
and the concrete platform
of a vacant rest stop

I don't remember which state
but it was the beginning
of a desert climate
grass browning with bare patches
cricket song
overwhelming

we were visiting relatives
a road trip to Texas from Seattle

even in my earliest tweens
I didn't like the idea
something not right about Texas
and Texans

I didn't know where
that prejudice came from

and being trapped
in the car the whole while
with my brother and Dad

at the time
the two least favorite people
in my life

but then
there was this gap
at this rest stop
on the boundary
between civilization and nature

inside
a tiny fieldmouse
nursing six even smaller pink blobs

as the sun began to set
and the crickets sang

v. what is what seems

some things I love

words in books
watching spiders build their webs
how clouds drift by
or transform
into impossible manifestations
the colors of crickets in flight
the curiosity of vines
conversations rivers have with pebbles
pebbles smoothed down to reveal patterns and designs
fossils yawning in sudden sunlight
wind making odd music
by itself
and with trees
a cat's indifference
when I try to entice it to come closer
little dogs snoring
moths and butterflies
frogs peeping loud
but unseen
koi in a pond world of their own
abstract shapes weeds choose to grow
rainbows and thunderstorms
the ocean and seashells
moss and Autumn leaves
hidden lives in the foliage
laughing people in restaurants
the smell of freshly baked bread

forget-me-not

I wonder
about all the places I've forgotten

do they still exist
or were they dreams to begin with
tiny blue Pentecostal flowers
rise as a reminder
faces I've seen
names on the tip of my tongue
landscapes of buildings   streets   trees
blur to a single vagary of past
with a few precious highlights
shining like stars
like the Milky Way

behind the door was

everything I dreamed about
when I was sick with longing

behind the door was
everything I feared would come to pass
in this world
filled with anger
and lust for power

behind the door
was my heart
breaking
china
tearing clothes
rolling in the shards

behind the door
was the monster
I wanted to be

behind the door
I could breathe again

behind the door
my mind was free
to wander
toward any light
I could imagine

behind the door
was a pile
of dead dry moths

trucks and truck parts

rust
like sad music
I've heard that some modern car paints
are actually a single giant molecule
don't know how that works
or what kind of music it would make
something synth and electronic
like a planetarium maybe
I've been places where trucks and truck parts
and construction equipment rust
all I heard was birdsong
the rustling of wind in trees
as the pink white salamanders
fled my eight-year-old grasping
I wonder if the truck parts
sing to each other
on rainy nights
if the pink white salamanders
dance in moonlight
I always thought
there was something magic
in places
where there are
no people

cages we choose

social isolation

gated communities

nine to five

freeways

poetry

a recipe

sometimes
words need to stew a while

to percolate
to pop and ping a bit
until the timer
dings
and the savor
and spice
have soaked thoroughly through

and despite
only being words
in your mind

you can taste them

smell the steamy aroma
of the perfect verb

roll the meaty texture
of the right noun
around your mouth

before writing them down

sometimes

the waiting

makes words
all the more filling

the angry onion

you give me a random line
and I'll give you a random line
you want to write about computers
I want to write about swords and adventure
      you say *forgiveness is divine*
I say your ice-cream
is a symbol
of the chaos inside my soul
it belongs on the floor
      you tell me to quiet my ego
I am a fox in I trap I yell
I am gnawing my own hand off
      you say *cellar-door*
      is the most beautiful word
      in the English language
and now I'm stumped
didn't I hear that in some movie once
I can't think of which one
so I am silent
and the silence gets heavier
it rushes in like a tsunami
I am drowning in it
and I've never been more frightened
but then
I see you
and the silence calms
becomes a still lake
      you just smile
and so do I

kittens

kittens think
the world
their play thing
and they are right

kittens nap
as if napping
were a divine gift
and they are right

kittens will love you
just because you are there

for a kitten
just existing
makes you worthy of love

except of course
if they think
you might be edible

a bird in the hand

frightened flutter
of a tiny heart
trying
to stay
as still
as possible

first
there was
the flutter
of wings

I thought
I imagined it

then
lying on the floor
playing late night video games

the air
of wing beats
against my foot
an uncertain
tweet

a sparrow
lost in a world of walls

I caught it
using a towel as a net
went to free it outside

hesitated
fascinated
by this warm

fragile thing
this life
I held in my hands

in the dark cool night

I let it go

as a poet

I know about circles
what begins
begins again
comes back
and is known
in the end

it's a little strange for me
going back
to the hospital
I was born in
for heart surgery

knowing
my mother died
in a recovery room
after surgery

as a poet
I know how words and sounds
repeat
build
to conclusions
come full circle
tension created
released
new circle
begins

I watch the world spin
hummingbirds
dine on foxglove
bees bumble from bloom to bloom

I know my anxiety
is more myth
than substance
and remind myself
of the amazing technology
the routineness of the procedure
and the expertise of the surgeon

she thought I had a medical background
I asked all the right questions
but no
I am just a poet
good with research
I notice patterns

and bees
yellow and black circles of buzz and fuzz

or perhaps
I am not worried enough

but going back
to the hospital
I was born in
a full circle
as a poet
how could I resist?

what is what seems

rain blurs reality

melts edges

reflects the unreal
into the real

or perhaps
what we think of as real
is the illusion

a hazy maze of thought and perception

external stimuli

may not be separate
but extensions of self

consciousness connects
what on the surface seems separate

underground
the mushroom is the forest
a single entity

what we see above
are merely blooms or pimples

the aspen grove a singular clone tree
repeated over and over
roots singular and connected

maybe in some quantum super cosmic sense
humans are the same way

all violence against others is violence against ourselves
all love given is love received

on this journey
we discover
we are already there

light unknown

light

from a time
we do not know

sparkles
in the void
of our consciousness

on this horizon
a stainless steel
obelisk
silhouettes
the Milky Way

it wasn't put here
by aliens

it wasn't put here
to be worshiped

it wasn't made
by gods
or faeries
or djinn

ordinary people
made it

ordinary people put it here
for no reason
other
than to remind us
the extraordinary

and wonderous
are not
so very
far
away

Wonderful World
after the song "What a Wonderful World,"
Louis Armstrong

smiling
not just with his whole face
not even with his whole body
but his voice
and every bit of his essence
was joy
a joy
he shared
still shares

I sometimes think
the problem with humanity
is humanity
we should evolve
beyond hate
beyond greed
become
beings of light
without want
but
then again
some of my best friends
are human

I also think
about some Buddhist ideas
I once read
that this world
is one half Heaven
one half Hell

a perfect balance
the perfect place
to learn all the lessons needed
to become a Buddha

but who cares about that
the sky is rumpled silver gray
vibrant greens
grow full of birdsong
and conversation
dogs play and run
even the Cessna
up above
loops about
for joy and training
today is a good day
to watch the ivy grow
search for four-leaf clovers
dance to wind chimes
order pizza
chat with friends
and just enjoy
being alive
at this moment
in this smiling world

shadow and light

in the darkness
inside me
there is a ringing sound
soft
almost a buzz
a chorus of bees
mesmerized
by dance
and flowers
only the gods can name
this vibration
is a light
in the darkness
a light
which includes darkness

bless me
for I have committed
acts worthy
of sainthood
sin
only in the eyes
of the sinful

forgive me
my existence
blasphemy
against angst
against despair
and in support
of despair
dripping of icicles
weeping
the arrival
of Spring

does the memory of water

stretch back
to the Pleistocene

does it remember
Precambrian
oddities
swimming in its soupy prime

does it remember
being steam
ice

does it remember
when we were all stardust

flying fast
from ourselves?

things to do while waiting for the apocalypse

buy a gun
learn to speak Swedish
take up knitting
and racquetball
get a job
pay bills
take up hula dancing
get a rabbit
name it Stewart
paint your garage
buy zombie insurance
watch the sun set
find a neat-looking rock
order a pizza
pet a stray cat
learn to use chopsticks
plant an onion
sell the gun
buy a hat

things I have forgotten

I have forgotten
the smell of petrichor
from the mossy weedy yard
just after a June rain

I forgot the mole mounds
and all the treasure
they push up into their slag heaps

I have forgotten the sound of human voices
birds singing
and rain in a rhythm
only an oracle can decipher

I have forgotten forgetting
forgot to water the cactus
forgot to say hello to the stray cat
the neighbor's dog
the crows watching me with indifferent eyes

I don't remember how frogs sing in the distance in Spring
or how cumulus roils up into castles and dragons across
    the sky

I don't remember the alphabet
or my times tables
or why I have this string tied to my finger

but one thing I will never forget
is what's-her-name
and whatever it was she did
that was so memorable

dandelions

will survive
the apocalypse

mosquitoes too
and ants
and nettles probably
but dandelions for sure

we've prepared them
with pesticides
herbicides
culled the weakest strains
created innovative ways
to kill off
all but the strongest
cleverest
of them
we've made sure
the legacy of the human species
after we are gone
will be dandelions

tonight

in the heartbeat
of the sea
I carved your name
in grains of sand
soon
the sky will clear
and stars
will fall to Earth
one photon
at a time
you told me once
to be prepared
for truth
but tonight
I can not
tell the difference
between reflection
and sky
between
you
and I

all through this night

I'm writing a treasure map
for you to follow
don't despair
I won't yell or torture you
its not a scam
I want you to frolic
through a pile of leaves
feel the empathy
of a pleasant pond
set up tent
on the curve of a crescent moon
I want to bestow on you
a window seat to wonder
diversify the spectrum
of forgotten self
make the invisible
visible
the cold
warm
to send you
on a journey
under the stars
to find
a sunbeam
and a strong verb
to guide you home
to your porch
and to another dream

Today's Sermon
after Cheryl Dumesnil

today's sermon is about
clovers in bloom
rust and freshly mowed grass
dandelions and honeysuckle
the heart still beats
the day is a rustling wind
a wind chimes day
a birds chirping
and iced tea day

today's sermon
is a kaleidoscopic view
of dirt
and the microscopic lives
making the foundation
of ecology

this day's sermon
is of gratitude
not blame
of hope
not hate

a sermon of poetry
player pianos
and friendship
the sky smiling and cooing

today's sermon
does not allow bullets
forbids bombs
is full to the buttercup brim
of live and let live

this sermon
is about kitchens
and open hands
bicycle rides
and red-winged blackbirds
and everywhere grace lives

today
is the sermon
calm yourself
let go of fear
and you may hear it

I don't have any answers

but the azure stripe
on the dragonfly's tail
seems to know
something

the sparrow
with the white patch on its back
flies away

the workmen next door
have stopped for lunch
the sounds of hammers
and electric saws
replaced
by a slow murmur
of silence

what I need most right now
is something I'll never have
perhaps this is true
for everyone

but still
we go on

teachers
teaching

plumbers
unclogging

doctors
mending
the brain

a finger
lungs
a pinky toe

and clear as a bell
or the woosh of wind
clouds pass by
and we find
we have all we need
in this moment
and the sparrow returns
to sing

about the author

Brendan McBreen was abandoned in suburbia and raised by men: a kind but patriarchal father and older brothers who mostly had their own lives. Before the divorce, Brendan's biggest influence was a woman called Mom who was an artist herself and encouraged Brendan's creativity with Salvador Dali, Vincent van Gogh, and Bob Ross.

In high school, Brendan tried hard to be male, dealt poorly with depression, anxiety, suicidal thoughts, and loneliness. Around this time poetry was discovered, along with denial. After they graduated, they got their black belt in karate and realized the necessity of being true to one's self. At which point they revisited an old term they previously avoided like the plague: *transgender*.

While this went on, there was writing, critique circles, workshops taught by poets with impressive bodies of work, attempts at college, counseling, collage art, exploring nature, meditation, dogs, cats, rain, rainbows, rivers, forests, oceans, beaches, 9/11s, 9 hour flights, a book of poetry from MoonPath Press (*Cosmic Egg*, 2017), Obama, Trump, an occasional really good pizza, a plan to transition from male to female, lacks of money, postponements, bills, tears, laughter, friends, family, and a bunch of other stuff.

Now there's this book! Hope you enjoy it. :)

www.ingramcontent.com/pod-product-compliance
Lightning Source LLC
Chambersburg PA
CBHW030152100526
44592CB00009B/238